Introduction

As a busy quilter, I'm always looking for shortcuts and projects that look hard but are actually easy. Precuts are one of my favorite shortcuts. Precut fabrics help to speed up the fabric selection process and create a scrappy-looking quilt with little to no work. In this book, you will find nine quick and easy quilts that can be made with your favorite fat quarter bundle or even a selection of fabrics from your stash.

My other favorite designing trick for creating quilts that look more complex than they are is the use of secondary designs. This is when you make one single block, but when you put the single blocks together, other designs show up. This is seen in Summer Chorus and Aurora Sky.

Scrappy doesn't always have to mean lots of different colors. A scrappy pattern can also use fabrics from one single color family. Twilight is a perfect example of this. The quilt was created using just whites, grays and blacks, but it would also look good in red and cream, or blue and white.

Go and grab your favorite fat quarters, and start sewing! Make quilting your voice.

—Scott A. Flanagan

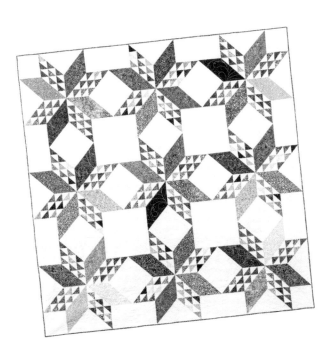

Table of Contents

Aurora Sky

Brightly colored bands of light mingle with solar winds, resulting in a beautiful display in the sky.

Skill Level
Confident Beginner

Finished Sizes
Quilt Size: 71" x 83"
Block Size: 12" x 12"
Number of Blocks: 30

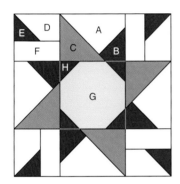

Star
12" x 12" Finished Block
Make 30

Materials
- 4¼ yards white print*
- 12 assorted fat quarters*
- 2 yards gray print*
- 2 yards blue print*
- 5½ yards backing*
- 79" x 91" batting*
- Thread
- Basic sewing tools and supplies

*Fabrics from the Expressions Batiks Express Yourself! Ombre collection from Riley Blake Designs; Warm & Natural: Warm 100 batting from The Warm Company used to make sample.

Project Notes
Read all instructions before beginning this project.

Stitch right sides together using a ¼" seam allowance unless otherwise specified.

Materials and cutting lists assume 40" of usable fabric width for yardage and 20" for fat quarters.

Arrows indicate directions to press seams.

WOF – width of fabric
HST – half-square triangle ◲
QST – quarter-square triangle ⊠

Cutting

From white print cut:

- 120 (4" x 5½") A rectangles
- 120 (2½" x 4") D rectangles
- 120 (2" x 4") F rectangles
- 8 (2" x WOF) strips, stitch short ends to short ends, then subcut into:
  2 (2" x 63½") I and 2 (2" x 72½") J border strips

From each of 6 assorted fat quarters cut:

- 3 (5½") G squares
- 8 (4") C squares**

From each of 6 assorted fat quarters cut:

- 2 (5½") G squares
- 12 (4") C squares**

From gray print cut:

- 120 (3") B squares
- 120 (2½") E squares
- 120 (2") H squares

From blue print cut:

- 8 (4½" x WOF) strips, stitch short ends to short ends, then subcut into:
  2 (4½" x 71½") K and 2 (4½" x 75½") L border strips
- 9 (2½" x WOF) binding strips

**Group assorted C squares into sets of four matching squares for a total of 30 matched sets. These will make the star points.

Completing the Blocks

1. Refer to Sew & Flip Flying Geese on page 7 and use four white A rectangles, four gray B squares and four matching assorted C squares to make four matching flying geese units (Figure 1). Repeat to make a total of 30 sets of four matching flying geese units.

Flying Geese Unit
Make 30 matching
sets of 4

Figure 1

2. Refer to Sew & Flip Corners on page 7 and sew a gray E square to a white D rectangle. Sew a white F rectangle to the long edge as shown to make a corner unit (Figure 2). Repeat to make a total of 120 corner units.

Corner Unit
Make 120

Figure 2

3. Refer again to Sew & Flip Corners and use gray H squares and assorted G squares to make 30 center units (Figure 3).

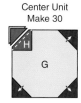

Center Unit
Make 30

Figure 3

4. Paying close attention to orientation, arrange four corner units, four matching flying geese units and one center unit into three rows as shown (Figure 4). Sew into rows and join the rows to complete a Star block. Make 30.

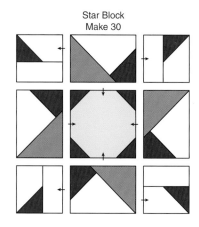

Star Block
Make 30

Figure 4

Completing the Quilt

1. Referring to the Assembly Diagram, lay out the blocks in six rows of five blocks each.

2. Sew the blocks into rows and join the rows to complete the quilt center. Press.

3. Sew the I–L border strips to the quilt top in alphabetical order.

4. Layer, baste, quilt as desired and bind referring to Quilting Basics. The photographed quilt was quilted with a large swirl design. ●

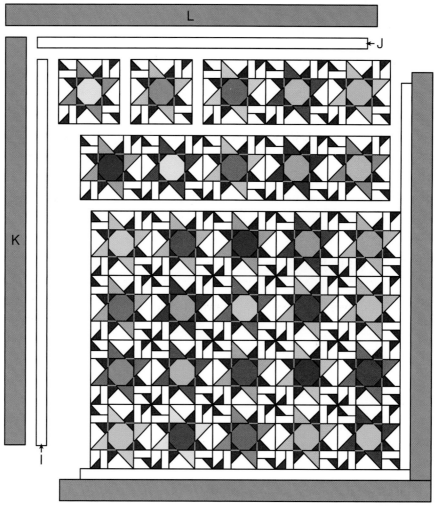

Aurora Sky
Assembly Diagram 71" x 83"

SEW & FLIP FLYING GEESE

With this method, squares are sewn onto opposite ends of a rectangle. The rectangle will be the center of the flying geese unit and the squares will become the "wings." After sewing in place, the squares are trimmed and flipped open to create the unit. The bias edges aren't exposed until after sewing so there is no concern about stretch and distortion.

Cutting

Refer to the pattern for the sizes to cut the rectangle and squares. Cut as directed in the pattern.

Determine the finished size of the flying geese unit you'd like to make and add ½" to the desired finished height and width of the flying geese unit, then cut a rectangle that size.

Cut two squares the same size as the height of the cut rectangle.

For example, to make one 2" x 4" finished flying geese unit, cut a 2½" x 4½" rectangle and two 2½" squares (Photo A).

Photo A

Assembly

1. Draw a diagonal line from corner to corner on the wrong side of each small square.

Place a square, right sides together, on one end of the rectangle. Sew just outside the drawn line (Photo B).

Photo B

2. Using a rotary cutter, trim ¼" away from sewn line.

Open and press to reveal the corner triangle or wing (Photo C).

Photo C

3. Place the second square, right sides together, on the opposite end of the rectangle. This square will slightly overlap the previous piece.

Sew just outside the drawn line and trim ¼" away from sewn line as before.

Open and press to complete the flying geese unit (Photo D).

Photo D

4. If desired, square up the finished unit to the required unfinished size. ●

SEW & FLIP CORNERS

Use this method to add triangle corners in a quilt block.

1. Draw a diagonal line from corner to corner on the wrong side of the specified square. Place the square, right sides together, on the indicated corner of the larger piece, making sure the line is oriented in the correct direction indicated by the pattern (Figure 1).

2. Sew on the drawn line. Trim ¼" away from sewn line (Figure 2).

3. Open and press to reveal the corner triangle (Figure 3).

Figure 1

Figure 2

Figure 3

4. If desired, square up the finished unit to the required unfinished size. ●

Picnic at the Fair

The air is filled with fun, excitement and cheerful laughter as you enjoy an outdoor meal at the fair.

Skill Level
Confident Beginner

Finished Sizes
Quilt Size: 54" x 64"
Block Size: 4½" x 8"
Number of Blocks: 96

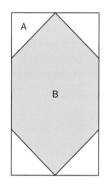

Dark
4½" x 8" Finished Block
Make 48

Light
4½" x 8" Finished Block
Make 48

Materials
- 3¼ yards low-volume background*
- 12 fat quarters assorted prints*
- ⅝ yard dark stripe*
- 3½ yards backing*
- 62" x 72" batting*
- Basic sewing tools and supplies

*Fabrics from the Bee Basics collection by Riley Blake Designs; Warm & Natural: Warm 100 batting from The Warm Company used to make sample.

Project Notes
Read all instructions before beginning this project.

Stitch right sides together using a ¼" seam allowance unless otherwise specified.

Materials and cutting lists assume 40" of usable fabric width for yardage and 20" for fat quarters.

Arrows indicate directions to press seams.

WOF – width of fabric
HST – half-square triangle ◹
QST – quarter-square triangle ⊠

Cutting

From low-volume background cut:
- 49 (5" x 8½") B rectangles
- 192 (2¾") A squares

From each assorted fat quarter cut:
- 4 (5" x 8½") B rectangles (48 total)
- 16 (2¾") A squares (192 total)

From dark stripe cut:
- 7 (2½" x WOF) binding strips

Completing the Blocks

1. Referring to Sew & Flip Corners on page 7, sew two assorted A squares to opposite corners of low-volume background B rectangles, noting directions to press seam allowances (Figure 1a). Repeat for remaining corners to make 48 Light blocks (Figure 1b).

a.

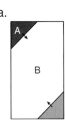

b.   Make 48

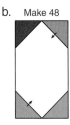

c.   Make 48

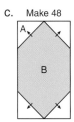

Figure 1

2. In the same manner, sew low-volume background A squares to assorted B rectangles, noting directions to press seam allowances, to complete 48 Dark blocks (Figure 1c).

Completing the Quilt

1. Referring to the Assembly Diagram, arrange and sew together the blocks in eight rows of 12 blocks each, alternating Light and Dark blocks.

2. Sew the rows together to complete the quilt top.

3. Layer, baste, quilt as desired and bind referring to Quilting Basics. The photographed quilt was quilted with an edge-to-edge design that combines geometric shapes and feathers. ●

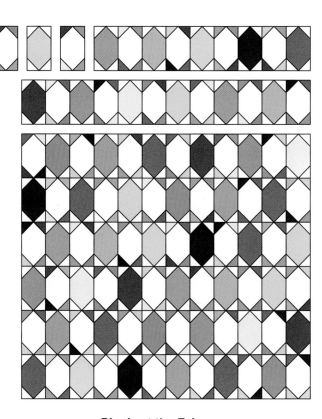

Picnic at the Fair
Assembly Diagram 54" x 64"

Twilight

In the midst of twilight's quietude, the first stars begin to twinkle, heralding the arrival of night.

Skill Level
Confident Beginner

Finished Sizes
Quilt Size: 59" x 71"
Block Size: 12" x 12"
Number of Blocks: 20

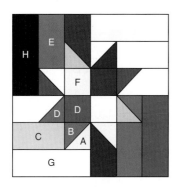

Star
12" x 12" Finished Block
Make 20

Materials
- 10–12 assorted light fat quarters*
- 10–12 assorted dark fat quarters*
- ½ yard light gray*
- 1⅔ yards black floral*
- 4½ yards backing fabric*
- 70" x 80" batting*
- Thread
- Basic sewing tools and supplies

*Fabrics from the Expressions Batiks Achromatic Dance collection by Riley Blake Designs; Warm & Natural: Warm 100 batting from The Warm Company used to make sample.

Project Notes
Read all instructions before beginning this project.

Stitch right sides together using a ¼" seam allowance unless otherwise specified.

Arrows indicate directions to press seams.

Materials and cutting lists assume 40" of usable fabric width for yardage and 20" for fat quarters.

WOF – width of fabric
HST – half-square triangle ◻
QST – quarter-square triangle ⊠

Cutting

From light fat quarters cut a total of:
- 40 (3") A squares
- 40 (2½" x 6½") G rectangles
- 80 (2½" x 4½") C rectangles
- 80 (2½") F squares

From dark fat quarters cut a total of:
- 40 (3") B squares
- 40 (2½" x 6½") H rectangles
- 80 (2½" x 4½") E rectangles
- 80 (2½") D squares

From light gray cut:
- 6 (2" x WOF) strips, sew short ends to short ends, then subcut into:
  2 (2" x 60½") I strips and 2 (2" x 51½") J strips

From black floral cut:
- 7 (4½" x WOF) strips, sew short ends to short ends, then subcut into:
  2 (4½" x 63½") K strips and 2 (4½" x 59½") L strips
- 7 (2½" x WOF) binding strips

Completing the Blocks

1. Referring to Half-Square Triangles, make 80 A-B units (Figure 1). Trim to measure 2½".

A-B Unit
Make 80

Figure 1

2. Referring to Sew & Flip Corners on page 7, use C rectangles and D squares to make a total of 40 C-D units (Figure 2). In the same way, use E rectangles and F squares to make a total of 40 E-F units.

C-D Unit
Make 40

E-F Unit
Make 40

Figure 2

3. Sew one C rectangle and one A-B unit into a row (Figure 3). Sew one C-D unit and one D square into a row. Sew rows together and sew one G rectangle to the top to make a light quarter star unit. Make 40.

Light Quarter
Star Unit
Make 40

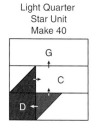

Figure 3

4. Sew one E rectangle and one A-B unit into a row (Figure 4). Sew one E-F unit and one F square into a row. Sew rows together and sew one H rectangle to the top to make a dark quarter star unit. Make 40.

Dark Quarter
Star Unit
Make 40

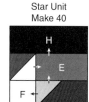

Figure 4

5. Lay out two each light and dark quarter star units into two rows of two (Figure 5). Sew into rows and join the rows to make a block. Make 20.

Make 20

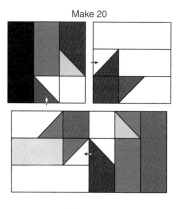

Figure 5

HALF-SQUARE TRIANGLES

Half-square triangles (HSTs) are a basic unit of quilting used in many blocks or on their own. This construction method will yield two HSTs.

1. Refer to the pattern for size to cut squares. The standard formula is to add ⅞" to the finished size of the square. Cut two squares from different colors this size. For example, for a 3" finished HST unit, cut 3⅞" squares.

2. Draw a diagonal line from corner to corner on the wrong side of the lightest color square. Layer the squares right sides together. Stitch ¼" on either side of the drawn line (Figure A).

Figure A

3. Cut the squares apart on the drawn line, leaving a ¼" seam allowance and making two HST units referring to Figure B.

Figure B

4. Open the HST units and press seam allowances toward the darker fabric making two HST units (Figure C). ●

Figure C

Completing the Quilt

1. Lay out the blocks into five rows of four blocks. Sew blocks into rows and join the rows to complete the quilt center.

2. Sew I strips to opposite sides of the quilt center. Sew J strips to the top and bottom.

3. Sew K strips to opposite sides of the quilt. Sew L strips to the top and bottom.

4. Layer, baste, quilt as desired and bind referring to Quilting Basics. The photographed quilt was quilted with an overall swirl design. ●

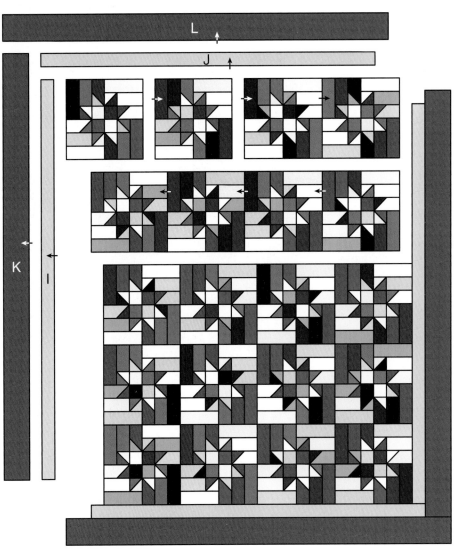

Twilight
Assembly Diagram 59" x 71"

Serenade & Splendor

The sweet and gentle melodies of spring crescendo
to vibrant summer symphonies.

Skill Level
Confident Beginner

Finished Sizes
Quilt Size: 65" x 65"
Block Size: 9" x 9"
Number of Blocks: 36

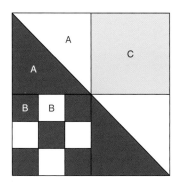

Block
9" x 9" Finished Block
Make 36

Materials
- 9 assorted print fat quarters*
- 1⅞ yards white solid*
- 1⅝ yards light teal print*
- 4⅜ yards backing*
- 73" x 73" batting*
- Basic sewing tools and supplies

*Fabrics from the Textured Spring Basics collection by Sandy Gervais for
Riley Blake Designs; Warm & Natural: Warm 100 batting from The Warm
Company used to make sample.*

Project Notes
Read all instructions before beginning this project.

Stitch right sides together using a ¼" seam
allowance unless otherwise specified.

Materials and cutting lists assume 40" of usable
fabric width for yardage and 20" for fat quarters.

Arrows indicate directions to press seams.

WOF – width of fabric
HST – half-square triangle ◻
QST – quarter-square triangle ◻

Cutting

From each assorted print fat quarter cut:
- 4 (5½") A squares
- 4 (5") C squares
- 20 (2") B squares

From white solid cut:
- 36 (5½") A squares
- 144 (2") B squares
- 6 (2" x WOF) inner border strips

From light teal print cut:
- 7 (4½" x WOF) outer border strips
- 7 (2½" x WOF) binding strips

Completing the Blocks & Sections

1. Refer to Half-Square Triangles on page 15 to make 36 matching pairs of HSTs using assorted print A squares and white solid A squares (Figure 1). Trim to 5".

Half-Square Triangles
Make 36 matching pairs

Figure 1

Here's a Tip

Lay out the blocks before sewing them together to make sure you have a color placement that is pleasing to your eye.

2. Lay out five matching print B squares and four white B squares (Figure 2). Join to make a nine-patch. Make 36 nine-patches.

Nine-Patch
Make 36

Figure 2

3. Sew together two matching HSTs, one matching nine-patch and one contrasting C square as shown to complete a block (Figure 3). Make 36 blocks total.

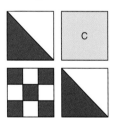

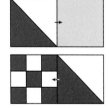

Block
Make 36

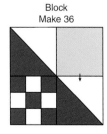

Figure 3

Completing the Quilt

1. Referring to the Assembly Diagram, lay out the blocks, paying close attention to the orientation of the blocks. Join the blocks into rows, then join the rows to complete the quilt center.

2. Sew the six white inner border strips along the short ends into one long strip.

3. Measure through the center of the quilt lengthwise and cut two D inner border strips to this length. Sew the D strips to left and right sides of quilt.

4. Measure through the center of the quilt widthwise and cut two E inner border strips to this length. Sew to top and bottom of quilt.

5. Repeat steps 2–4 with the seven light teal border strips, creating two F strips and two G strips. Sew the F strips to the left and right sides of quilt. Sew the G strips to top and bottom.

6. Layer, baste, quilt as desired and bind referring to Quilting Basics. The photographed quilt was quilted with a feather design. ●

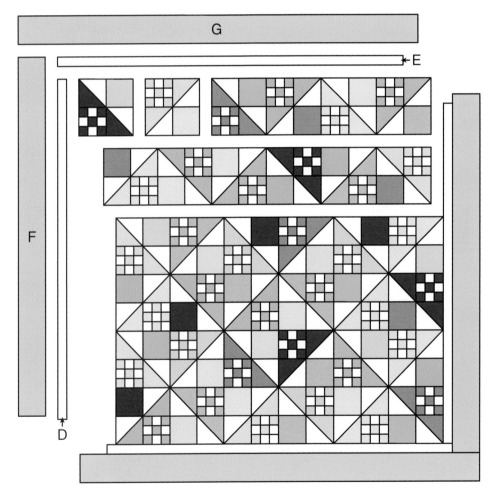

Serenade & Splendor
Assembly Diagram 65" x 65"

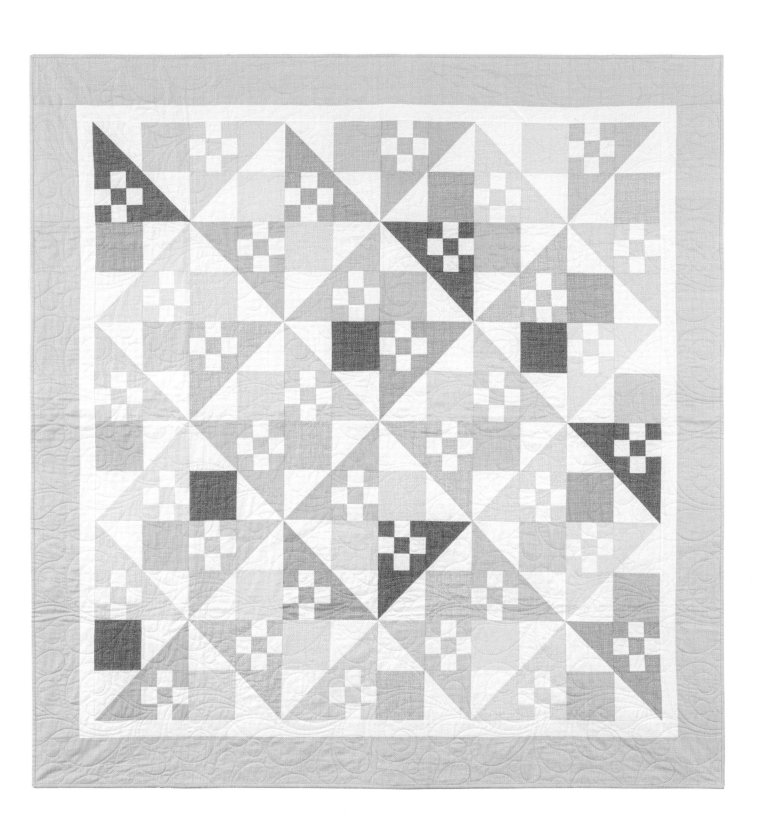

Summer Chorus

Enjoy the warmth of bright summer skies
filled with vibrant and colorful stars.

Skill Level
Confident Beginner

Finished Sizes
Quilt Size: 60½" x 75"
Block Size: 12" x 12"
Number of Blocks: 20

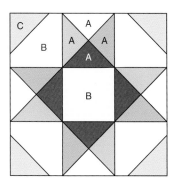

Star
12" x 12" Finished Block
Make 20

Materials
- 3 yards background solid*
- 20 fat quarters assorted prints*
- ⅔ yard stripe*
- 5 yards backing*
- 68" x 83" batting*
- Basic sewing tools and supplies

Fabrics from the Here Comes the Sun collection by Sandy Gervais for Riley Blake Designs; Warm & Natural: Warm 100 batting from The Warm Company used to make sample.

Project Notes
Read all instructions before beginning this project.

Stitch right sides together using a ¼" seam allowance unless otherwise specified.

Materials and cutting lists assume 40" of usable fabric width for yardage and 20" for fat quarters.

Arrows indicate directions to press seams.

WOF – width of fabric
HST – half-square triangle ◻
QST – quarter-square triangle ⊠

Cutting

From background solid cut:
- 20 (5½") A squares, then cut diagonally twice ⊠
- 80 (4½") B squares
- 49 (3" x 9½") D rectangles

From each assorted fat quarter cut:
- 3 (5½") A squares, then cut diagonally twice (60 total) ⊠
- 1 (4½") B square (20 total)
- 4 (3½") C squares (80 total)
- 5 (2" x 3") F rectangles (100 total)

From leftover fat quarters cut:
- 30 (3") E squares

From stripe cut:
- 8 (2½" x WOF) binding strips

Completing the Blocks

1. Arrange one background solid A triangle and three contrasting A triangles as shown (Figure 1a). Sew triangles together in pairs; join the pairs to make one star point unit (Figure 1b). Trim unit to 4½" x 4½". Repeat to make 20 sets of four matching star point units.

a.

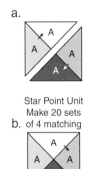

Star Point Unit
Make 20 sets
b. of 4 matching

Figure 1

2. Referring to Sew & Flip Corners on page 7, use C squares and background solid B squares to make 80 corner units (Figure 2).

Corner Unit
Make 80

Figure 2

3. Referring to the Star block diagram, arrange one set of four star point units, four matching corner units and one contrasting B square in three rows as shown. Sew units and square together in rows; join the rows to complete one block. Make 20.

Completing the Sashing

1. Sew two F rectangles to the short ends of one D rectangle to complete one sashing unit (Figure 3). Make 49.

Sashing Unit
Make 49

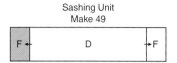

Figure 3

2. Referring to the Assembly Diagram, arrange and sew together five E squares alternating with four sashing units into one sashing row. Make six.

Completing the Quilt

1. Referring to the Assembly Diagram, arrange and sew together five sashing units alternating with four Star blocks as shown to make one block row. Make five.

2. Sew together sashing rows and block rows as shown to complete the quilt top.

3. Layer, baste, quilt as desired and bind referring to Quilting Basics. The photographed quilt was quilted with a Baptist fan design. ●

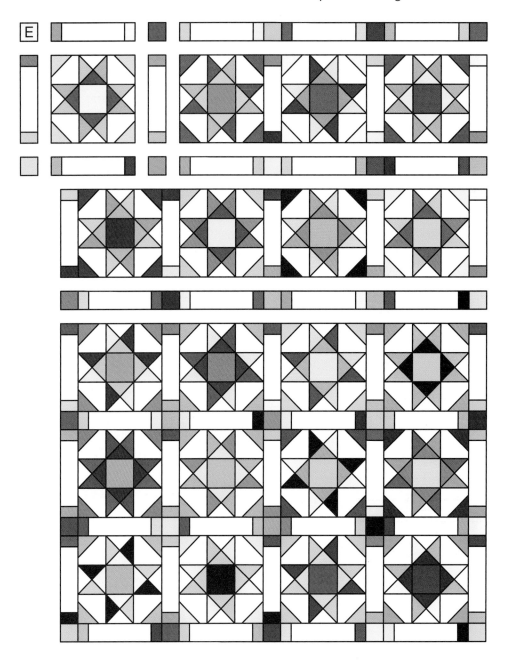

Summer Chorus
60½" x 75"

Meadow & Memories

The gentle breeze carries the sweet scent of fanciful wildflowers, their resplendent blooms painting a picturesque landscape of grace and beauty.

Skill Level
Confident Beginner

Finished Sizes
Quilt Size: 60" x 75"
Block Size: 15" x 15"
Number of Blocks: 20

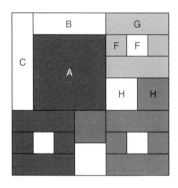

Block A
15" x 15" Finished Block
Make 10

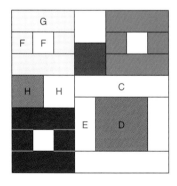

Block B
15" x 15" Finished Block
Make 10

Materials
- 2 yards white print*
- 20 assorted fat quarters*
- ¾ yard dark print*
- 5 yards backing*
- 68" x 83" batting*
- Thread
- Basic sewing tools and supplies

*Fabrics from the Chalk & Charcoal collection from Riley Blake Designs; Warm & Natural: Warm 100 batting from The Warm Company used to make sample.

Project Notes

Read all instructions before beginning this project.

Stitch right sides together using a ¼" seam allowance unless otherwise specified.

Materials and cutting lists assume 40" of usable fabric width for yardage and 20" for fat quarters.

Arrows indicate directions to press seams.

WOF – width of fabric
HST – half-square triangle ◻
QST – quarter-square triangle ⊠

Cutting

From white print cut:

- 40 (3½") H squares
- 30 (2½" x 9½") C rectangles
- 10 (2½" x 7½") B rectangles
- 20 (2½" x 5½") E rectangles
- 60 (2½") F squares

From each of 10 assorted fat quarters cut:

- 1 (7½") A square
- 2 (3½") H squares
- 6 (2½" x 6½") G rectangles
- 6 (2½") F squares

From each of 10 assorted fat quarters cut:

- 1 (5½") D square
- 2 (3½") H squares
- 6 (2½" x 6½") G rectangles
- 6 (2½") F squares

From dark print cut:

- 8 (2½" x WOF) binding strips

Completing the Blocks

1. Sew a white B rectangle to the right edge of an assorted A square. Sew a white C rectangle to the top edge to complete unit A (Figure 1). Repeat to make a total of 10 unit A.

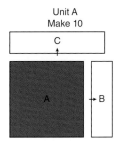

Figure 1

2. Sew white E rectangles to opposite edges of an assorted D square. Sew white C rectangles to top and bottom edges to complete unit B (Figure 2). Repeat to make a total of 10 unit B.

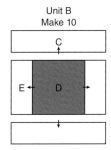

Figure 2

3. Sew matching assorted F squares to opposite edges of a white F square. Sew matching assorted G rectangles to top and bottom edges to complete unit C (Figure 3). Repeat to make a total of 60 unit C.

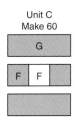

Figure 3

4. Sew together a white H square and an assorted H square to make unit D (Figure 4). Repeat to make a total of 40 unit D.

Unit D
Make 40

Figure 4

5. Sew together one unit A, three unit C and two unit D as shown to make Block A (Figure 5). Repeat to make a total of 10 Block A.

Block A
Make 10

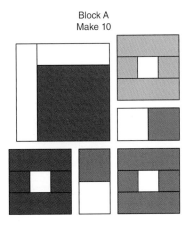

Figure 5

6. Sew together one unit B, three unit C and two unit D as shown to make Block B (Figure 6). Repeat to make a total of 10 Block B.

Block B
Make 10

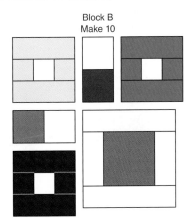

Figure 6

Completing the Quilt

1. Referring to the Assembly Diagram, lay out the blocks in five rows of four blocks each.

2. Sew the blocks into rows and join the rows to complete the quilt center. Press.

3. Layer, baste, quilt as desired and bind referring to Quilting Basics. The photographed quilt was quilted with an overall leaf design. ●

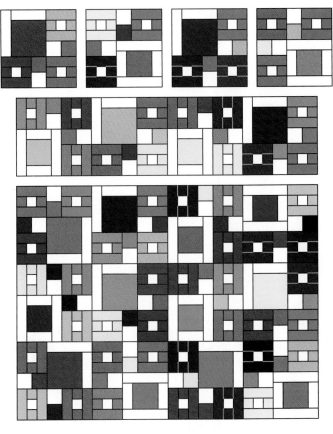

Meadow & Memories
Assembly Diagram 60" x 75"

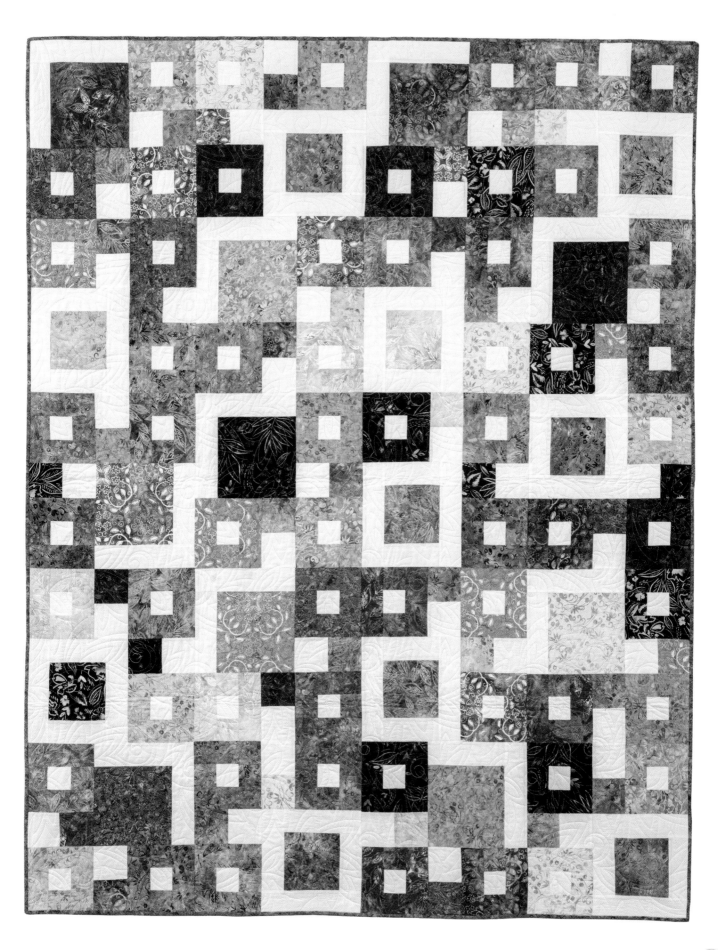

Weekend Wanderer

Seek out new places and experiences as you embrace
the spirit of adventure in spontaneous getaways.

Skill Level
Confident Beginner

Finished Sizes
Quilt Size: 71" x 83"
Block Size: 12" x 12"
Number of Blocks: 30

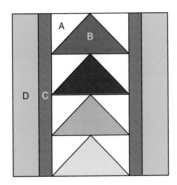

Flying Geese
12" x 12" Finished Block
Make 30

Materials
- 3 yards cream print*
- 15 fat quarters assorted prints*
- 1 yard brown print*
- 1⅞ yards blue floral*
- 5½ yards backing*
- 79" x 91" batting*
- Basic sewing tools and supplies

*Fabrics from the Autumn collection by Lori Holt for Riley Blake Designs;
Warm & Natural: Warm 100 batting from The Warm Company used to
make sample.

Project Notes
Read all instructions before beginning this project.

Stitch right sides together using a ¼" seam
allowance unless otherwise specified.

Materials and cutting lists assume 40" of usable
fabric width for yardage and 20" for fat quarters.

Arrows indicate directions to press seams.

WOF – width of fabric
HST – half-square triangle ◻
QST – quarter-square triangle ⊠

Cutting

From cream print cut:
- 7 (2" x WOF) strips, stitch short ends to short ends,
  then subcut into:
  2 (2" x 72½") E and 2 (2" x 63½") F border strips
- 240 (3½") A squares

From each of 15 fat quarters cut:
- 8 (3½" x 6½") B rectangles
- 4 (2½" x 12½") D rectangles

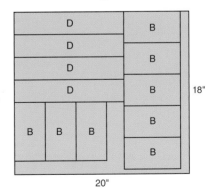

Fat Quarter
Cutting Diagram

From brown print cut:
- 60 (1½" x 12½") C rectangles

From blue floral cut:
- 8 (4½" x WOF) strips, stitch short ends to short ends, then subcut into:
  - 2 (4½" x 75½") G and 2 (4½" x 71½") H border strips
- 9 (2½" x WOF) binding strips

Completing the Blocks

1. Refer to Sew & Flip Flying Geese on page 7 and use the A squares and B rectangles to make 120 flying geese units (Figure 1).

Flying Geese Unit
Make 120

Figure 1

2. Join four flying geese units as shown to make a flying geese strip (Figure 2). Make 30.

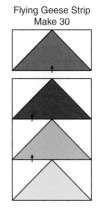

Flying Geese Strip
Make 30

Figure 2

3. Sew C rectangles to the long sides of a flying geese strip (Figure 3). Add matching print D rectangles to complete a Flying Geese block. Make 30 total.

Make 30

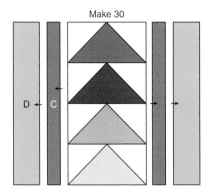

Figure 3

Completing the Quilt

1. Referring to the Assembly Diagram, lay out the blocks in six rows of five blocks each, noting the orientation of the blocks.

2. Sew the blocks into rows and join the rows to complete the quilt center. Press.

3. Sew the E–H border strips to the quilt top in alphabetical order.

4. Layer, baste, quilt as desired and bind referring to Quilting Basics. The photographed quilt was quilted with an edge-to-edge swirl design. ●

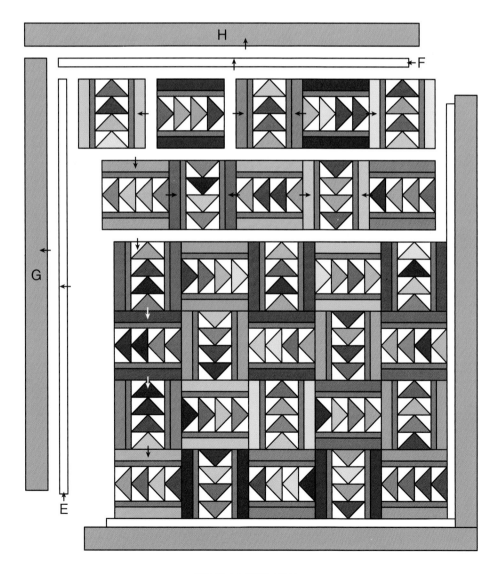

Weekend Wanderer
Assembly Diagram 71" x 83"

The Road Home

Peace and solace meet like old friends on a journey,
weaving through landscapes both familiar and strange
with promises of rest at home on the horizon.

Skill Level
Confident Beginner

Finished Sizes
Quilt Size: 86" x 98"
Block Size: 12" x 12"
Number of Blocks: 42

Materials
- 21 fat quarters assorted batiks*
- 3⅛ yards cream batik*
- ½ yard rust batik*
- 2½ yards dark green batik*
- 8⅓ yards backing*
- 94" x 106" batting*
- Basic sewing tools and supplies

Fabrics from the Expressions Batiks Warm Rain collection from Riley Blake Designs; Warm & Natural: Warm 100 batting from The Warm Company used to make sample.

Project Notes
Read all instructions before beginning this project.

Stitch right sides together using a ¼" seam allowance unless otherwise specified.

Materials and cutting lists assume 40" of usable fabric width for yardage and 20" for fat quarters.

Arrows indicate directions to press seams.

WOF – width of fabric
HST – half-square triangle
QST – quarter-square triangle

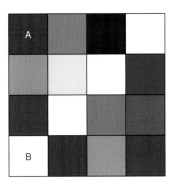

Chain
12" x 12" Finished Block
Make 21

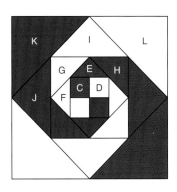

Snail's Trail
12" x 12" Finished Block
Make 21

Cutting

From each fat quarter cut:
- 1 (7¼") J square, then cut twice diagonally
- 1 (6⅞") K square, then cut once diagonally
- 1 (4¼") E square, then cut twice diagonally
- 1 (3⅞") H square, then cut once diagonally
- 12 (3½") A squares
- 2 (2") C squares

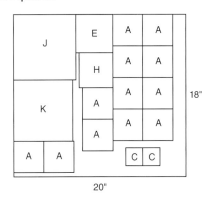

Fat Quarter
Cutting Diagram

From cream batik cut:

- 11 (7¼") I squares, then cut twice diagonally
- 21 (6⅞") L squares, then cut once diagonally
- 11 (4¼") F squares, then cut twice diagonally
- 21 (3⅞") G squares, then cut once diagonally
- 84 (3½") B squares
- 42 (2") D squares

From rust batik cut:

- 8 (2" x WOF) strips, stitch short ends to short ends, then subcut into:
  - 2 (2" x 84½") M and 2 (2" x 75½") N border strips

From dark green batik cut:

- 9 (6" x WOF) strips, stitch short ends to short ends, then subcut into:
  - 2 (6" x 87½") O and 2 (6" x 86½") P border strips
- 10 (2½" x WOF) binding strips

Completing the Blocks

1. Arrange and sew four rows using 12 assorted A squares and four cream B squares (Figure 1). Join the rows to complete a Chain block. Make 21 Chain blocks total.

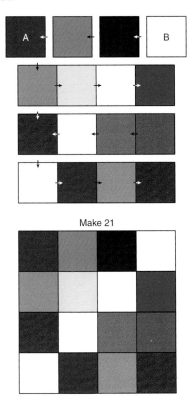

Make 21

Figure 1

2. For each Snail's Trail block, select two contrasting sets of the following batik pieces:

- 1 C square
- 1 E triangle
- 1 H triangle
- 1 J triangle
- 1 K triangle

You will also need the following cream pieces for each block:

- 2 D squares
- 2 F triangles
- 2 G triangles
- 2 I triangles
- 2 L triangles

You will have two E and two J triangles from each fat quarter and two F and two I triangles from the cream batik left over.

3. Using the contrasting C squares and the cream D squares for the first block, sew two rows of two squares each (Figure 2a). Join the rows. The unit should measure 3½" square from raw edge to raw edge.

a.

b.

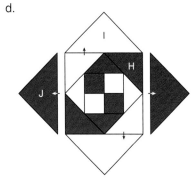

c.

d.

e.

Make 21

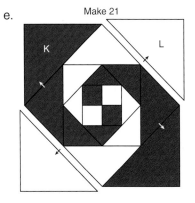

Figure 2

4. Sew contrasting E triangles to opposite sides, watching fabric placement carefully (Figure 2b). Sew cream F triangles to the remaining sides. The unit should measure 4¾" square.

5. Sew cream G triangles to opposite sides, watching placement (Figure 2c). Join contrasting H triangles to the remaining sides, watching fabric placement. The unit should measure 6½" square.

6. Sew cream I triangles to opposite sides (Figure 2d). Add contrasting J triangles to the remaining sides, watching fabric placement. The unit should measure 9" square.

7. Add contrasting K triangles to opposite sides, watching fabric placement (Figure 2e). Sew cream L triangles to the remaining sides to complete a Snail's Trail block measuring 12½" square. Make 21 Snail's Trail blocks total.

Completing the Quilt

1. Referring to the Assembly Diagram, lay out the blocks in seven rows of six blocks each, noting the placement of the blocks.

2. Sew the blocks into rows and join the rows to complete the quilt center. Press.

3. Sew the M–P border strips to the quilt top in alphabetical order.

4. Layer, baste, quilt as desired and bind referring to Quilting Basics. The photographed quilt was quilted with an edge-to-edge swirl design. ●

The Road Home
Assembly Diagram 86" x 98"

The Gathering

Open up to wonders of the heart as you gather, reflect and savor the moments of true beauty and the tranquil harmony of nature.

Skill Level
Confident Beginner

Finished Sizes
Quilt Size: 90" x 90"
Block Size: 30" x 30"
Number of Blocks: 9

Materials
- 10 assorted blue fat quarters*
- 10 assorted brown fat quarters*
- ⅞ yard binding fabric*
- 6 yards white tonal*
- 9 yards backing fabric*
- 100" x 100" batting*
- Thread
- Basic sewing tools and supplies

Fabrics from the Terrazzo Rocky Mountain and Terrazzo Frosty collections from Riley Blake Designs; Warm 100 batting from The Warm Company used to make sample.

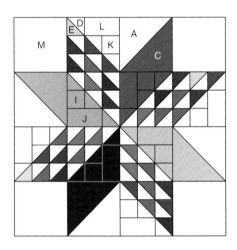

Blue Star
30" x 30" Finished Block
Make 5

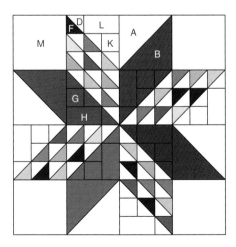

Brown Star
30" x 30" Finished Block
Make 4

Project Notes

Read all instructions before beginning this project.

Stitch right sides together using a ¼" seam allowance unless otherwise specified.

Arrows indicate directions to press seams.

Materials and cutting lists assume 40" of usable fabric width for yardage and 20" for fat quarters.

WOF – width of fabric
HST – half-square triangle ◺
QST – quarter-square triangle ◩

Cutting

From each blue fat quarter cut:

- 1 (8½") C square
- 3 (7") F squares
- 2 (3" x 5½") J rectangles
- 2 (3") I squares

From each of eight brown fat quarters cut:

- 1 (8½") B square
- 3 (7") E squares
- 2 (3" x 5½") H rectangles
- 2 (3") G squares

From each of remaining two brown fat quarters cut:

- 3 (7") E squares

From binding fabric cut:

- 10 (2½" x WOF) binding strips

From white tonal cut:

- 18 (8½") A squares
  36 (8") M squares
- 60 (7") D squares
- 36 (3" x 5½") L rectangles
- 36 (3") K squares

Completing the Blocks

1. Referring to Half-Square Triangles on page 15, make 16 A-B units (Figure 1). In the same way, make 20 A-C units. Trim all units to measure 8".

Figure 1

2. Referring to Eight-at-a-Time Half-Square Triangles, make 228 D-E units and 204 D-F units (Figure 2). Trim all units to measure 3". **Note:** *The eight-at-a-time technique will yield additional units; save for another project.*

Figure 2

EIGHT-AT-A-TIME HALF-SQUARE TRIANGLES

Half-square triangles (HSTs) are a basic unit of quilting used in many blocks or on their own. This construction method will yield eight HST units.

1. Refer to the pattern for size to cut squares. The standard formula is to add 1" to the finished size of the square then multiply by 2. Cut two squares from different colors this size. For example, for a 3" finished HST unit, cut 8" squares (3" + 1" = 4"; 4" x 2 = 8").

2. Draw two diagonal lines from corner to corner on the wrong side of the lightest color square. Layer the squares right sides together. Stitch ¼" on either side of both drawn lines (Figure A).

Figure A

3. Cut the sewn squares in half horizontally and vertically, making four squares. Then cut each square apart on the drawn line, leaving a ¼" seam allowance and making eight HST units referring to Figure B. Trim each HST unit to the desired size (3½" in this example).

Figure B

4. Open the HST units and press seam allowances toward the darker fabric making eight HST units (Figure C). ●

Figure C

3. Lay out three D-F units and three matching D-E units, one G square and one H rectangle into three rows (Figure 3). Sew into rows and join rows to make a brown center unit. Make 16. In the same way, use three D-E units and three matching D-F units, one I square and one J rectangle to make a blue center unit. Make 20.

Brown Center Unit
Make 16

Blue Center Unit
Make 20

Figure 3

4. Lay out six D-E units, one K square and one L rectangle into three rows (Figure 4). Sew into rows and join rows to make a brown outer unit. Make 20. In the same way, use six D-F units, one K square and one L rectangle to make a blue outer unit. Make 16.

Brown Outer Unit
Make 20

Blue Outer Unit
Make 16

Figure 4

5. Lay out one blue outer unit, one brown center unit, one A-B unit and one M square into two rows of two (Figure 5). Sew into rows and join the rows to make one brown quarter unit. Make 16. In the same way, use one blue center unit, one brown outer unit, one A-C unit and one M square to make one blue quarter unit. Make 20.

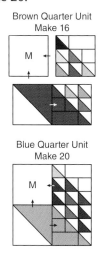

Brown Quarter Unit
Make 16

Blue Quarter Unit
Make 20

Figure 5

6. Lay out four brown quarter units into two rows (Figure 6). Sew into rows and join the rows to make a Brown Star block. Make four. In the same way, lay out four blue quarter units to make a Blue Star block. Make five.

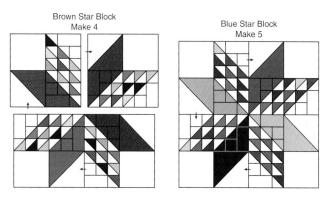

Brown Star Block
Make 4

Blue Star Block
Make 5

Figure 6

Completing the Quilt

1. Lay out the blocks into three rows of three blocks each, alternating blocks. Sew blocks into rows and join the rows to complete the quilt top.

2. Layer, baste, quilt as desired and bind referring to Quilting Basics. The photographed quilt was quilted with an overall feather design. ●

The Gathering
Assembly Diagram 90" x 90"

Quilting Basics

The following is a reference guide. For more information, consult a comprehensive quilting book.

Quilt Backing & Batting

Cut your backing and batting 8" larger than the finished quilt-top size and 4" larger for quilts smaller than 50" square. **Note:** *Check with longarm quilter about their requirements, if applicable. For baby quilts not going to a longarm quilter 4"–6" overall may be sufficient.* If preparing the backing from standard-width fabrics, remove the selvages and sew two or three lengths together; press seams open. If using 108"-wide fabric, trim to size on the straight grain of the fabric. Prepare batting the same size as your backing.

Quilting

1. Press quilt top on both sides and trim all loose threads. **Note:** *If you are sending your quilt to a longarm quilter, contact them for specifics about preparing your quilt for quilting.*
2. Mark quilting design on quilt top. Make a quilt sandwich by layering the backing right side down, batting and quilt top centered right side up on flat surface and smooth out. Baste layers together using pins, thread basting or spray basting to hold. **Note:** *Tape or pin backing to surface to hold taut while layering and avoid puckers.*
3. Quilt as desired by hand or machine. Remove pins or basting as you quilt.
4. Trim batting and backing edges even with raw edges of quilt top.

Binding the Quilt

1. Join binding strips on short ends with diagonal seams to make one long strip; trim seams to ¼" and press seams open (Figure 1).

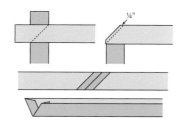

Figure 1

2. Fold ½" of one short end to wrong side and press. Fold the binding strip in half with wrong sides together along length, again referring to Figure 1; press.
3. Starting about 3" from the folded short end, sew binding to quilt top edges, matching raw edges and using a ¼" seam. Stop stitching ¼" from corner and backstitch (Figure 2).

Figure 2

4. Fold binding up at a 45-degree angle to seam and then down even with quilt edges, forming a pleat at corner (Figure 3).

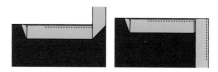

Figure 3

5. Resume stitching from corner edge as shown in Figure 3, down quilt side, backstitching ¼" from next corner. Repeat, mitering all corners, stitching to within 3" of starting point.
6. Trim binding, leaving enough length to tuck inside starting end and complete stitching (Figure 4).

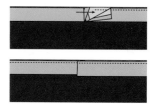

Figure 4

7. If stitching binding by hand, machine-sew binding to the front of the quilt and fold to the back before stitching. If stitching by machine, machine-sew binding to back of the quilt and fold to the front before stitching.

Supplies

We would like to thank the following manufacturers who provided materials to our designers to make sample projects for this book.

Aurora Sky, page 3: Fabrics from the Expressions Batiks Express Yourself! Ombre collection from Riley Blake Designs; Warm & Natural: Warm 100 batting from The Warm Company.

Picnic at the Fair, page 8: Fabrics from the Bee Basics collection by Riley Blake Designs; Warm & Natural: Warm 100 batting from The Warm Company.

Twilight, page 12: Fabrics from the Expressions Batiks Achromatic Dance collection by Riley Blake Designs; Warm & Natural: Warm 100 batting from The Warm Company.

Serenade & Splendor, page 17: Fabrics from the Textured Spring Basics collection by Sandy Gervais for Riley Blake Designs; Warm & Natural: Warm 100 batting from The Warm Company.

Summer Chorus, page 23: Fabrics from the Here Comes the Sun collection by Sandy Gervais for Riley Blake Designs; Warm & Natural: Warm 100 batting from The Warm Company.

Meadow & Memories, page 27: Fabrics from the Chalk & Charcoal collection from Riley Blake Designs; Warm & Natural: Warm 100 batting from The Warm Company.

Weekend Wanderer, page 32: Fabrics from the Autumn collection by Lori Holt for Riley Blake Designs; Warm & Natural: Warm 100 batting from The Warm Company.

The Road Home, page 37: Fabrics from the Expressions Batiks Warm Rain collection from Riley Blake Designs; Warm & Natural: Warm 100 batting from The Warm Company.

The Gathering, page 41: Fabrics from the Terrazzo Rocky Mountain and Terrazzo Frosty collections from Riley Blake Designs; Warm & Natural: Warm 100 batting from The Warm Company.

ISBN: 979-8-89253-373-7

3 4 5 6 7 8 9